Easy Christmas Cut-up Cakes

Easy Christmas Cut-up Cakes

MELISSA BARLOW

PHOTOGRAPHS BY ZAC WILLIAMS

GIBBS SMITH
TO ENRICH AND INSPIRE HUMANKIND

First Edition
22 21 20 19 18   5 4 3 2 1

Text © 2018 Melissa Barlow
Photographs © 2018 Zac Williams

Published by
Gibbs Smith
P.O. Box 667
Layton, Utah 84041

1.800.835.4993 orders
www.gibbs-smith.com

Designed by Kate Frances Design
Printed and bound in Hong Kong

Gibbs Smith books are printed on either recycled, 100% post-consumer
waste, FSC-certified papers or on paper produced from sustainable PEFC-
certified forest/controlled wood source. Learn more at www.pefc.org.

Library of Congress Cataloging-in-Publication Data

Names: Barlow, Melissa, author.
Title: Easy Christmas cut-up cakes / Melissa Barlow.
Description: Layton, Utah : Gibbs Smith, [2018]
Identifiers: LCCN 2018000365 | ISBN 9781423650362
(jacketless hardcover)
Subjects: LCSH: Christmas cooking. | Cake. | LCGFT: Cookbooks.
Classification: LCC TX739.2.C45 B37 2018 | DDC 641.5/686—
dc23 LC record available at https://lccn.loc.gov/2018000365

For my mom, Nancy,
who lifts my spirits all year long.

Contents

Introduction

This book is full of easy cake ideas that you can make for any special winter holiday occasion—especially Christmas. Choose your favorite pattern and surprise your family and friends with your creative genius!

Bake the Cake

The first step when making any cake in this book is to read the entire recipe before starting. Make sure you have the right pans for the cake you've chosen and gather all the ingredients together so they will be handy.

Preheat the oven while you grease the cake pans and mix the batter. An oven that has been preheated will cook the cake evenly. And pans that have been greased will let the cake pop out in one piece after it has cooled a bit.

Follow the instructions on the cake mix package for ingredients. After mixing the ingredients together and making a smooth batter, carefully transfer the batter to the greased pans. Place the pans in the oven and bake for the time listed in the recipe. To test for doneness, insert a toothpick in the center of the cake. If it comes out clean, the cake is done.

Let the cakes cool completely before you frost them. This will help keep crumbs out of your frosting. You can even bake the cake a day before you frost it.

Frost the Cake

Frosting is one of the most important parts of decorating your cake. Frosting can be messy, so proceed with patience.

To help keep your cake plate clean, stick little pieces of wax paper just under the edges of your cake. When you finish frosting the cake, pull out the wax paper pieces and throw them away.

What Frosting Should I Use?

There are many store-bought frostings that taste great and will work just fine with these recipes. Some of these purchased frostings are whipped, making them easier to spread, however, sometimes you need frosting that is stiffer, like for squeezing through a decorating bag to draw lines or make shapes. For stiffer frosting (or if you want to flavor the frosting yourself), you can make your own frosting using the provided recipes.

How Do I Decorate with Frosting?

If you use one of the homemade frosting recipes (pages 14–15) you can put it into a decorator's bag and use special tips to make shapes like dots, stars, and flowers. You can also buy decorating icing that comes in tubes at the grocery store or craft store. You might want to use these instead of decorator's bags. They are great to use for decorating and adding details to your cakes, and you can often screw on decorator's tips. The tubes come in small and large sizes. The small tubes are usually filled with gel frosting and the large tubes with decorating icing. Both come in all kinds of colors and are very easy to use.

How Do I Color My Frosting?

Most grocery stores carry food-coloring kits usually located where you'll find cake mixes. These work well, but sometimes the colors aren't as deep or as dark as you'd like them to be. You may want to go to a craft store and buy some specialty gel, paste, or powder icing colors such as the Wilton brand. They are not expensive and will help you get the exact color you need. If there isn't a craft store near you that carries these products, some chain stores like Wal-Mart do, or you can also purchase icing colors online.

Add small amounts of food coloring to homemade frosting or store-bought frosting, stirring until you get the color you want.

Decorating the Cake

Now comes the best part. You can choose to decorate your cake with your favorite candy and other treats. You don't have to use exactly what is listed in each recipe. You can make substitutions if you can't find the cookies or candies listed, keeping in mind that it's best to use bright, colorful candy for the best looking results.

The most important thing is to be creative and have fun. The possibilities are endless!

Vanilla Buttercream Frosting

MAKES ABOUT 2 CUPS

½ cup butter, softened*
3 to 4 tablespoons water
  or milk
2 teaspoons vanilla
Pinch salt, optional
3 to 4 cups powdered sugar

Beat butter, water or milk, and vanilla together with an electric hand mixer until smooth. Add salt if using. Gradually beat in the sugar, 1 cup at a time. If the frosting is too thick, add more water or milk by the teaspoon until it reaches the right consistency. If it is too thin, add a little more sugar.

Note: Substitute 1 cup regular vegetable shortening and clear vanilla if you want a pure white frosting.

Chocolate Buttercream Frosting

MAKES ABOUT 2 CUPS

½ cup butter, softened
3 to 4 tablespoons water
  or milk
2 teaspoons vanilla
Pinch salt, optional
½ cup cocoa powder
3 to 4 cups powdered sugar

Beat butter, water or milk, and vanilla together with an electric hand mixer until smooth. Add salt if using. Beat in cocoa powder. Gradually beat in the sugar, 1 cup at a time. If the frosting is too thick, add more water or milk by the teaspoon until it reaches the right consistency. If it is too thin, add a little more sugar.

The Cakes

Candy Cane

SERVES 10 TO 12

Pans

1 (8-inch) round pan
1 (8-inch) square pan

Cake

1 (15.25-ounce) box white
  cake mix
1 recipe Vanilla Buttercream
  Frosting (page 14) or 1
  (16-ounce) can white frosting
Fruit by the Foot
Red licorice ropes or
  red M&Ms

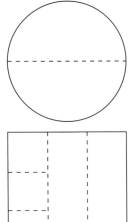

Preheat oven to 350 degrees. Prepare pans with nonstick cooking spray.

Make cake mix according to package directions. Evenly divide the batter between both pans. Bake for 27–32 minutes, or until a toothpick inserted in the center comes out clean; remove from oven. Cool cake in pans for 10 minutes, and then invert and cool completely on a wire rack.

Cut the cakes according to the diagrams.

On a large serving platter or foil-wrapped board, stack the 2 round halves on top of each other to create a two-layer cake, frosting between the layers. Stack the 2 long strips together with frosting in between. Position the strip to make the long part of the candy cane. Stack the 2 smaller squares to finish off the "hook." You can eat or throw away the unused piece.

Frost the entire cake smoothly with remaining frosting. Press the Fruit by the Foot and licorice or red M&Ms on the candy cane to create the stripes.

Smiley Snowman

SERVES 10 TO 12

Bowls

1 (1.5-quart) ovenproof glass
bowl
1 (1-quart) ovenproof glass
bowl

Cake

1 (15.25-ounce) box cake mix,
any flavor
1 recipe Vanilla Buttercream
Frosting (page 14) or 1
(16-ounce) can white frosting
Yogos Rollers or Fruit by
the Foot
Peanut M&Ms
1 tube black decorating icing
1 baby carrot
Black licorice

Preheat oven to 350 degrees. Prepare the glass bowls with nonstick cooking spray.

Make cake mix according to package directions. Place $2/3$ of the batter into the 1.5-quart bowl and the remaining batter into the 1-quart bowl. Bake for 27–32 minutes, or until a wooden skewer inserted into the center of the smaller cake comes out clean; remove from oven. Continue baking the larger cake another 5–10 minutes, or until a wooden skewer inserted into the center comes out clean; remove from oven. Cool cake in bowls for 10 minutes, and then invert and cool completely on a wire rack.

Cut the larger cake according to the diagram. Place the cakes on a large serving platter or foil-wrapped board to create the snowman.

Frost the entire cake with white frosting. Make a scarf using the Yogos Rollers or Fruit by the Foot. Gently press the

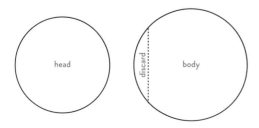

Continued . . .

Smiley Snowman

M&Ms into the snowman's belly for buttons, and cut small pieces of black licorice to make his smile.

Use the black icing to draw the circles of the snowman's eyes and then stick a small piece of black licorice in each for the pupils. Finally, finish by sticking in his carrot nose and licorice arms.

Variation: You can use chocolate chips in place of the licorice for his mouth and eyes.

Sweet Angel

SERVES 10 TO 12

Pans

1 (8-inch) round pan
1 (8-inch) square pan

Cake

1 (15.25 ounce) box cake mix,
   any flavor
1 recipe Vanilla Buttercream
   Frosting (page 14) or
   1 (16-ounce) can white
   frosting, divided, ½ left
   white
About ½ cup pink or peach
   frosting
About ½ cup brown frosting
1 tube red decorating icing
   or gel

Preheat oven to 350 degrees. Prepare pans with nonstick cooking spray.

Make cake mix according to package directions. Divide batter evenly between each pan. Bake for 27–32 minutes, or until a toothpick inserted in the center comes out clean; remove from oven. Cool cake in pans for 10 minutes, and then invert and cool completely on a wire rack.

Cut the square cake according to the diagram. Place the cakes on a large serving platter or foil-wrapped board to create the angel and her wings.

Frost the angel's body and wings smoothly with the white frosting. Frost the round cake smoothly with the pink or peach frosting.

Using a decorator's bag with a round tip, give the angel curly hair by piping the brown frosting in swirls on top of

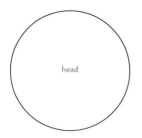

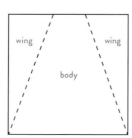

Continued . . .

Sweet Angel

her head; add the eyes and eyelashes. Use the red icing to pipe a mouth.

Place the remaining white frosting in a decorator's bag with a star tip, and pipe a halo onto her head as shown in the photo and outline her body.

Variation: Add colorful sprinkles to the angel's wings.

Peppermint Candy

SERVES 10 TO 12

Pans

1 (9-inch) round pan
1 (8-inch) square pan

Cake

1 (15.25-ounce) box cherry
   chip cake mix
1 recipe Vanilla Buttercream
   Frosting (page 14) or 1
   (16-ounce) can white frosting
Red sprinkles
1 tube red decorating icing

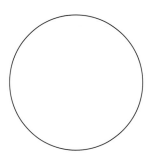

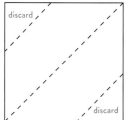

Preheat oven to 350 degrees. Prepare pans with nonstick cooking spray.

Make cake mix according to package directions. Put 2½ cups of the batter in the round pan and the remaining batter in the square pan. Bake for 27–32 minutes, or until a toothpick inserted in the center comes out clean; remove from oven. Cool cake in pans for 10 minutes, and then invert and cool completely on a wire rack.

Cut the square cake according to the diagram. Arrange the cakes on a large serving platter or foil-wrapped board in the shape as shown in the photo.

Frost the entire cake smoothly with white frosting. Using a piece of scratch paper, draw a 9-inch circle and cut it into "pie" wedges. Set the cutouts on top of the round cake; then remove every other one. Cover the parts of the frosting that are showing with a thick layer of red sprinkles. Press down gently with your fingers to make sure the sprinkles stay in place, and then remove the remaining pieces of paper. Using the red icing, outline the candy as shown in the photo.

Variation: Use a chocolate cake mix and crushed peppermint candies instead of red sprinkles.

Gingerbread Man

SERVES 10 TO 12

Pan

9 x 13-inch pan

Cake

**1 (15.25-ounce) box chocolate
cake mix**
**1 recipe Chocolate
Buttercream Frosting
(page 15) or 1 (16-ounce)
can chocolate frosting**
**½ cup white frosting, or 1 tube
white decorating icing**
**1 tube black decorating icing
or gel**
M&Ms or gumdrops

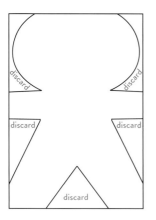

Preheat oven to 350 degrees. Prepare pan with nonstick cooking spray.

Make cake mix according to package directions. Pour batter into pan. Bake for 27–32 minutes, or until a toothpick inserted in the center comes out clean; remove from oven. Cool cake in pan for 10 minutes, and then invert and cool completely on a wire rack.

Cut the cake according to the diagram. Place the cake on a large serving platter or foil-wrapped board. Frost the entire cake smoothly with the chocolate frosting.

Using a decorator's bag with a round or star tip, outline the entire gingerbread man and pipe on his face, using white frosting for the eyes and black icing for the pupils. Make dots for his buttons, and decorate his arms and legs. Finish decorating by using M&Ms or gumdrops.

Toy Train

SERVES 8 TO 10

Pans

5 mini loaf pans

Cake

**1 (15.25-ounce) box cake mix,
any flavor**
**1 recipe Vanilla Buttercream
Frosting (page 14) or**
**1 (16-ounce) can white
frosting, divided, ½ colored
red and ½ colored green**
1 tube white decorating icing
16 Oreo cookies
1 plain ice cream cone
**White cotton candy or mini
marshmallows**
Red and green M&Ms
Christmas candies

Preheat oven to 350 degrees. Prepare pans with nonstick cooking spray.

Make cake mix according to package directions. Evenly divide the batter into each pan. Bake for 20–23 minutes, or until a toothpick inserted in the center comes out clean; remove from oven. Cool cake in pans for 10 minutes, and then invert and cool completely on a wire rack.

Cut 1 cake in half as shown in the diagram. Position one of the halves on top of another cake to make the engine. Discard or eat the other half. Place the engine on a large serving platter or foil-wrapped board, followed by the remaining cakes.

Frost the engine red and then pipe on the windows with the white frosting. Press 2 Oreos into the frosting on each side of the engine to make the wheels.

Frost the next car red, the next green, and the last one green. Press 2 Oreos into each side of the cars to make the wheels.

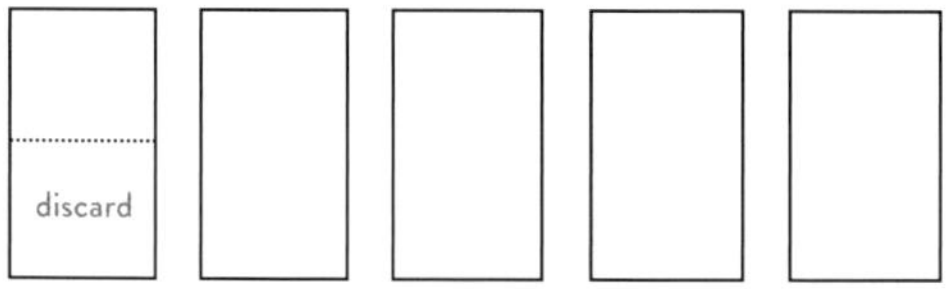

discard

Continued . . .

Toy Train

Frost the ice cream cone red and position on the front of the engine. (You may need to cut part of the cake away so it sits securely.) Place some cotton candy or mini marshmallows on top to look like smoke.

Stick M&Ms in the center of each Oreo wheel with a little frosting. Decorate the rest of the cars by loading them up with Christmas candies.

Variation: Use black licorice to connect the cars.

Toy Drum

SERVES 10 TO 12

Pans

2 (8-inch) round pans

Cake

1 (15.25-ounce) box cake mix, any flavor
1 recipe Vanilla Buttercream Frosting (page 14) or
1 (16-ounce) can white frosting, divided, 1/3 left white and 2/3 colored light green
Red and green M&Ms
1 tube red decorating icing or red string licorice
2 pieces red licorice
2 white Christmas Whoppers

Preheat oven to 350 degrees. Prepare pans with nonstick cooking spray.

Make cake mix according to package directions. Divide the batter evenly between the pans. Bake for 27–32 minutes, or until a toothpick inserted in the center comes out clean; remove from oven. Cool cake in pans for 10 minutes, and then invert and cool completely on a wire rack. Level the tops of each cake round; discard or eat the excess.

Place 1 cake cut side up on a large serving platter or foil-wrapped board and, using some of the white frosting, frost the top only. Once you have finished frosting the top, place the second cake cut side down over the frosting. (This will make it easier to frost because then you won't have to deal with the crumbs from cutting the cake level.)

Frost only the top of the cake with remaining white frosting. Frost the side of the cake smoothly with the green frosting so it touches the white from the top.

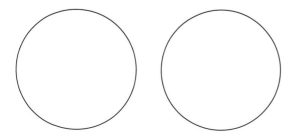

Continued . . .

Toy Drum

Place the M&Ms around the top and bottom of the cake. Using the red icing, pipe the lines around the sides of the drum as shown in the photo, or cut several pieces of red string licorice into equal lengths and use to create the zigzag lines.

Cut the tip off one end of each piece of licorice, dab a little white frosting on the cut end, and lay the licorice across the drum. Stick a Whopper on each of the frosted ends.

O Christmas Tree

SERVES 10 TO 12

Pan

9 x 13-inch pan

Cake

1 (15.25-ouncd) box chocolate cake mix
1 recipe Vanilla Buttercream Frosting (page 14) or
1 (16-ounce) can white frosting, colored light green
1 King-Size Snickers or Milky Way bar
1 tube red decorating icing
Red Peanut M&Ms

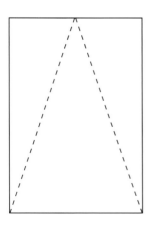

Preheat oven to 350 degrees. Prepare pan with nonstick cooking spray.

Make cake mix according to package directions. Pour batter evenly into pan. Bake for 27–32 minutes, or until a toothpick inserted in the center comes out clean; remove from oven. Cool cake in pan for 10 minutes, and then invert and cool completely on a wire rack.

Cut the cake according to the diagram. On a large serving platter or foil-wrapped board, position the 2 smaller triangle pieces together to create one large triangle, and spread a layer of green frosting over top. Place the large triangle on top and then frost the entire cake smoothly with remaining green frosting.

Cut the candy bar in half and stack the pieces together to make the tree trunk. Press them gently into the frosting at the bottom of the tree.

Use the red icing and a star tip to pipe a garland on the tree. Finish by decorating with M&Ms or other Christmas candies as desired.

Santa's Hat

SERVES 10 TO 12

Pans

Muffin pan or 1 small ramekin

9 x 13-inch pan

Cake

1 (15.25-ounce) box cake mix, any flavor

1 recipe Vanilla Buttercream Frosting (page 14) or 1 (16-ounce) can white frosting, divided, ⅔ colored red and ⅓ left white

White miniature marshmallows

Red sprinkles, optional

Preheat oven to 350 degrees. Prepare 1 muffin cup or the ramekin and the 9 x 13-inch pan by spraying with nonstick cooking spray.

Make cake mix according to package directions. Fill the muffin cup ⅔ full with batter and pour the remaining batter into the 9 x 13-inch pan. Bake for 17–20 minutes, or until a toothpick inserted into the center of the cupcake comes out clean; remove muffin pan. Continue baking the large cake 10–13 minutes, or until a toothpick inserted into the center comes out clean; remove from oven. Cool cupcake and cake in pans for 10 minutes, and then invert and cool completely on a wire rack.

Cut the cake according to the diagram. On a large serving platter or foil-wrapped board, position the two smaller triangle pieces together to create one large triangle and then spread a layer of red frosting over the top. Place the large triangle on top and use remaining red frosting to frost all but one strip at the bottom. Frost the bottom strip white, as well as the top and sides of the cupcake. Place the cupcake at the point of the hat.

Completely cover the cupcake and white strip on the hat with marshmallows. Top the red part of the hat with sprinkles, if desired.

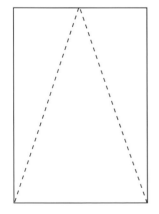

Snowflake Stocking

SERVES 10 TO 12

Pan
9 x 13-inch pan

Cake
1 (15.25-ounce) box cake mix, any flavor
1 recipe Vanilla Buttercream Frosting (page 14) or
1 (16-ounce) can white frosting, divided, ⅔ colored light blue and ⅓ left white
Blue sprinkles, optional
White miniature marshmallows

Preheat oven to 350 degrees. Prepare pan with nonstick cooking spray.

Make cake mix according to package directions. Pour batter evenly into pan. Bake for 27–32 minutes, or until a toothpick inserted in the center comes out clean; remove from oven. Cool cake in pan for 10 minutes, and then invert and cool completely on a wire rack.

Cut the cake according to the diagram. On a large serving platter or foil-wrapped board, position the rectangle piece at the top of the stocking.

Frost the stocking smoothly with the blue frosting and the rectangle part with the white frosting. Decorate the blue frosting with blue sprinkles, if desired. Completely cover the white frosting with the marshmallows.

Put some white frosting in a decorator's bag with a small round tip and pipe on the snowflakes; adding the marshmallows as shown in the photo.

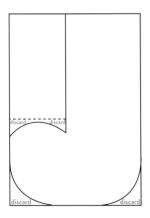

Star

SERVES 10 TO 12

Pan

1 (8-inch) square pan

Cake

1 (15.25-ounce) box lemon or
yellow cake mix
1 recipe Vanilla Buttercream
Frosting (page 14) or
1 (16-ounce) can white
frosting, colored light yellow
Yellow sprinkles

Preheat oven to 350 degrees. Prepare pan with nonstick cooking spray.

Make cake mix according to package directions. Pour batter evenly into pan. Bake for 27–32 minutes, or until a toothpick inserted in the center comes out clean; remove from oven. Cool cake in pan for 10 minutes, and then invert and cool completely on a wire rack.

Cut the cake according to the diagram. On a large serving platter or foil-wrapped board, position the 2 skinny top pieces to make the top point of the star. Flip over the fatter triangles and position to make the side points of the star. The side pieces will be pointing slightly upwards.

Frost the entire cake smoothly with yellow frosting, reserving about ½ cup. Tint the reserved frosting a darker yellow or orange color. Using a decorator's bag with a star tip, outline the star with the dark yellow frosting and then decorate with sprinkles.

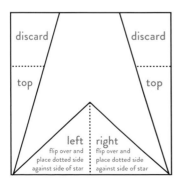

Fuzzy Mitten

SERVES 10 TO 12

Pan

9 x 13-inch pan

Cake

1 (15.25-ounce) box cake mix, any flavor
1 recipe Vanilla Buttercream Frosting (page 14) or 1 (16-ounce) can white frosting, divided, ⅓ left white, ⅔ colored light pink
Shredded sweetened coconut
Rainbow nonpareil sprinkles

Preheat oven to 350 degrees. Prepare pan with nonstick cooking spray.

Make cake mix according to package directions. Pour batter evenly into pan. Bake for 27–32 minutes, or until a toothpick inserted in the center comes out clean; remove from oven. Cool cake in pan for 10 minutes, and then invert and cool completely on a wire rack.

Cut the cake according to the diagram and then place the mitten on a large serving platter or foil-wrapped board. Discard or eat the leftover cake pieces.

Frost a strip across the bottom of the mitten with white frosting and frost the rest of the mitten pink.

Completely cover the white frosting with the coconut, pressing lightly to secure. Lightly sprinkle more coconut and nonpareils over the pink frosting.

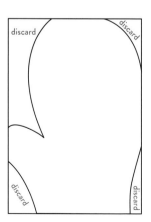

Wreath

SERVES 10 TO 12

Pan
Bundt pan

Cake
1 (15.25-ounce) box cake mix, any flavor
1 recipe Vanilla Buttercream Frosting (page 14) or
1 (16-ounce) can white frosting, divided, ½ colored light green, ½ colored dark green
Fruit by the Foot
Red Peanut M&Ms

Preheat oven to 350 degrees. Prepare pan with nonstick cooking spray.

Make cake mix and bake in pan according to package directions until done; remove from oven. Cool cake in pan for 10 minutes, and then invert and cool completely on a wire rack.

Place the cake on a serving platter or foil-wrapped board and frost entirely with light green frosting.

Using a decorator's bag with a star tip and the light green frosting, pipe on "pine needles" starting in the center ring and working your way out. Pipe over the entire wreath leaving spaces that will be filled in with the dark green frosting.

Using another decorator's bag with the same size star tip and dark green frosting, fill in any spaces so the entire cake is covered. Finish by making a bow with the Fruit by the Foot and adding M&Ms for holly berries; press each decoration gently into the frosting.

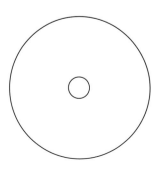

Red-Nosed Reindeer

SERVES 10 TO 12

Pans

2 (9-inch) round pans

Cake

1 (15.25-ounce) box cake mix, any flavor

1 recipe Vanilla Buttercream Frosting (page 14) or 1 (16-ounce) can white frosting, divided, 2/3 colored light brown, 1/3 colored dark brown

1 tube white decorating icing

2 dark brown M&Ms

1 tube red decorating icing

Preheat oven to 350 degrees. Prepare pans with nonstick cooking spray.

Make cake mix according to package directions. Divide batter evenly between the pans. Bake for 27–32 minutes, or until a toothpick inserted in the center comes out clean; remove from oven. Cool cake in pans for 10 minutes, and then invert and cool completely on a wire rack.

Cut the cakes according to the diagrams. Place the cake on a large serving platter or foil-wrapped board to create the reindeer and his antlers.

Frost the reindeer's face and ears (part of the antler cake) with the light brown frosting. Frost the antlers with the dark brown frosting.

Use the white icing to create the eyes and M&Ms for his pupils. Finally, use the red icing to make a big red nose.

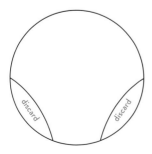
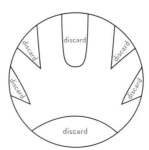

Penguin

SERVES 10 TO 12

Pans

Muffin pan
9 x 13-inch pan

Cake

1 (15.25-ounce) box cake mix,
  any flavor
1 recipe Vanilla Buttercream
  Frosting (page 14) or
  1 (16-ounce) can white
  frosting, divided, ⅓ colored
  black and ⅔ left white
1 tube yellow decorating icing

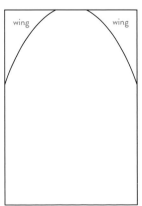

Preheat oven to 350 degrees. Prepare 2 muffin cups and the 9 x 13-inch pan with nonstick cooking spray.

Make cake mix according to package directions. Fill the 2 muffin cups ⅔ full with batter and then pour remaining batter into the 9 x 13-inch pan. Bake for 17–20 minutes, or until a toothpick inserted into the center of a cupcake comes out clean; remove from oven. Continue baking the large cake 10–13 minutes, or until a toothpick inserted into the center comes out clean; remove from oven. Cool cupcakes and cake in pans for 10 minutes, and then invert and cool completely on a wire rack.

Cut the cake according to the diagram. Place the cake on a large serving platter or foil-wrapped board to create the penguin and his wings.

Frost the wings and around the edge of the cake with the black frosting as shown in the photo. Fill in the center of the penguin and bottom edge with white frosting. Completely frost the cupcakes with yellow icing and then position as the penguin's feet.

Using a decorator's bag with a small round tip and remaining black frosting, outline the eyes and fill in the pupils. Use more yellow frosting to make the penguin's beak.

Ornament

SERVES 10 TO 12

Pan

9 x 13-inch pan

Cake

1 (15.25-ounce) box cake mix, any flavor

1 recipe Vanilla Buttercream Frosting (page 14) or 1 (16-ounce) can white frosting, divided, ¾ left white and ¼ colored bright green

Bright pink sprinkles

Bright green sprinkles

1 piece green licorice

Preheat oven to 350 degrees. Prepare pan with nonstick cooking spray.

Make cake mix according to package directions. Pour batter evenly into pan. Bake for 27–32 minutes, or until a toothpick inserted in the center comes out clean; remove from oven. Cool cake in pan for 10 minutes, and then invert and cool completely on a wire rack.

Cut the cake according to the diagram. Place the cake on a large serving platter or foil-wrapped board to create the ornament, piecing the 2 larger cut pieces into a square at the top for the ornament cap.

Frost the entire cake smoothly with white frosting. Using a decorator's bag with a small round tip and the green frosting, outline the pattern of the ornament. Fill in the stripes and diamond shapes with the sprinkles as desired. Finish by sticking the green licorice into the top of the cake to make the hanger.

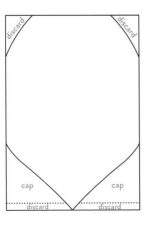

Little Gift

SERVES 20 TO 24

Pans

2 (8-inch) square pans

Cake

2 (15.25-ounce) boxes white or
 chocolate cake mixes
1 recipe Vanilla Buttercream
 Frosting (page 14) or 1
 (16-ounce) can white frosting
Red Fruit by the Foot
Red and green plain M&Ms

Preheat oven to 350 degrees. Prepare pans with nonstick cooking spray.

Make cake mixes according to package directions. Divide batter evenly between the pans and bake for 33–38 minutes, or until a toothpick inserted into the center comes out clean. Cool cake in pans for 10 minutes, and then invert and cool completely on a wire rack.

Level each cake top so they can be evenly stacked. Place 1 cake on a large square serving platter, or foil-wrapped board. Spread a layer of white frosting over top. Place the second cake on top and frost the entire cake white.

Position the Fruit by the Foot to look like ribbon and a bow around the gift. Finish by dotting the cake with M&Ms.

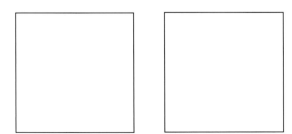

Elf Socks

SERVES 10 TO 12

Pan

9 x 13-inch pan

Cake

1 (15.25-ounce) box cake mix, any flavor
1 recipe Vanilla Buttercream Frosting (page 14) or
1 (16-ounce) can white frosting, divided, ½ colored brown and ½ colored pink
2 white Christmas Whoppers

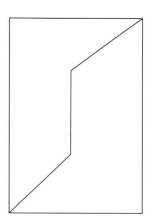

Preheat oven to 350 degrees. Prepare pan with nonstick cooking spray.

Make cake mix according to package directions. Pour batter evenly into pan. Bake for 27–32 minutes, or until a toothpick inserted in the center comes out clean; remove from oven. Cool cake in pan for 10 minutes, and then invert and cool completely on a wire rack.

Cut the cake according to the diagram. On a large serving plate or foil-wrapped board, position the 2 socks with the toes pointing out.

Very lightly frost each sock brown. Using 2 decorator's bags with the same size star tip, fill one bag with brown frosting and the other with pink frosting. Make stripes by piping rows of stars, about 4 or 5 deep of each color. This will make the socks look like they were knitted. Place a Whopper on the tip of each toe.

The North Pole

SERVES 10 TO 12

Pans

Muffin pan or 1 ramekin
1 (8-inch) square pan

Cake

1 (15.25-ounce) box cherry chip cake mix
1 recipe Vanilla Buttercream Frosting (page 14) or 1 (16-ounce) can white frosting, divided, 2/3 left white and 1/3 colored red
1 piece black licorice
1 tube black decorating icing

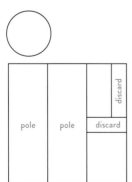

Preheat oven to 350 degrees. Prepare 1 muffin cup or the ramekin and the square pan with nonstick cooking spray.

Make cake mix according to package directions. Fill the muffin cup 2/3 full with batter. Pour the remaining batter into the square pan. Bake for 17–20 minutes, or until a toothpick inserted into the center of the cupcake comes out clean; remove from oven. Continue baking the large cake 10–13 minutes, or until a toothpick inserted into the center comes out clean; remove from oven. Cool cupcake and cake in pans for 10 minutes, and then invert and cool completely on a wire rack.

Cut the cake according to the diagram. On a large serving platter or foil-wrapped board, position the 2 long pieces end to end to create the pole.

Frost the entire pole smoothly with the white frosting. Use the red frosting to frost the cupcake and then place it at the top of the pole. In a decorator's bag with a round tip and red frosting, pipe the lines that wrap around the pole. Let the lines dry a little and then flatten with your finger.

Frost the smaller rectangle cake red for the post and attach it to the pole. Frost the remaining rectangle with the white frosting for the sign. Connect the sign to the post using pieces of licorice. Use the black icing to pipe the words "North Pole" on the sign.

Old-Fashioned Christmas Lightbulb

SERVES 10 TO 12

Pan

9 x 13-inch pan

Cake

1 (15.25-ounce) box cake mix, any flavor
1 recipe Vanilla Buttercream Frosting (page 14) or
1 (16-ounce) can white frosting, divided, ¾ colored red (or color of choice) and ¼ colored black
Black licorice
Sprinkles, optional

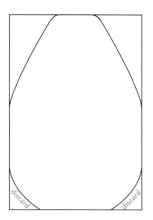

Preheat oven to 350 degrees. Prepare pan with nonstick cooking spray.

Make cake mix according to package directions. Pour batter evenly into pan. Bake for 27–32 minutes, or until a toothpick inserted in the center comes out clean; remove from oven. Cool cake in pan for 10 minutes, and then invert and cool completely on a wire rack.

Cut the cake according to the diagram. On a large serving platter or foil-wrapped board, position the 2 triangle pieces together to make a square (you may have to cut them a little so they fit together to make a rectangle). Place at the bottom of the lightbulb.

Frost the lightbulb smoothly with the red frosting and the square at the bottom with the black frosting. Cut licorice the same length as the bottom of the bulb and place on top to make the threads. Add sprinkles if desired.

Holly Berry

SERVES 10 TO 12

Pans

Muffin pan
1 (8-inch) square pan

Cake

1 (15.25-ounce) box cake mix, any flavor
1 recipe Vanilla Buttercream Frosting (page 14) or 1 (16-ounce) can white frosting, reserve ½ cup and color it red, color the rest light green
1 tube dark green decorating icing or gel

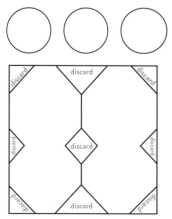

Preheat oven to 350 degrees. Prepare 3 muffin cups and the square pan with nonstick cooking spray.

Make cake mix according to package directions. Fill the 3 muffin cups ⅔ full with batter; pour remaining batter into square pan. Bake for 17–20 minutes, or until a toothpick inserted into the center of a cupcake comes out clean; remove from oven. Continue baking the large cake 10–13 minutes, or until a toothpick inserted into the center comes out clean; remove from oven. Cool cupcakes and cake in pans for 10 minutes, and then invert and cool completely on a wire rack.

Cut the square cake according to the diagram. Place the cupcakes on a large serving platter or foil-wrapped board for the holly berries and position the cake leaves. Frost the cupcakes red and the leaves light green. Outline the leaves with the dark green icing or green decorating gel.

Gingerbread House

SERVES 10 TO 12

Pans

2 (8-inch) square pans

Cake

1 (15.25-ounce) box cake mix,
  any flavor
1 recipe Vanilla Buttercream
  Frosting (page 14) or
1 (16-ounce) can white
  frosting, divided, ½ colored
  brown, ½ left white
4 whole graham crackers
Christmas candies

Preheat oven to 350 degrees. Prepare pans with nonstick cooking spray.

Make cake mix according to package directions. Pour ⅔ of the batter into 1 pan and the remaining ⅓ into the other pan. This will make 1 cake twice as thick as the other. Bake for 18–20 minutes, or until a toothpick inserted into the center of the thinner cake comes out clean; remove from oven. Continue baking the thicker cake 10–12 minutes more, or until a toothpick inserted into the center comes out clean; remove from oven. Cool cake in pans for 10 minutes and then invert and cool completely on a wire rack.

Cut the thinner cake into triangles according to the diagram, making sure it is level and completely flat. Cut the thicker cake in half according to the diagram and level. Stack the 2 long rectangles to form the base of the house on a large serving platter or foil-wrapped board, and use some of the brown frosting to frost between the layers. Stack and frost

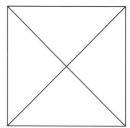

Continued . . .

Gingerbread House

the thin triangles together with white frosting and reinforce with toothpicks, if necessary, so they stay together to form the roof. Place on top of the house base.

Frost the rooftop with white frosting and the rest of the house with brown frosting. Place the graham crackers on top of the roof and then frost a thick layer of white frosting over the crackers, making sure to cover all the edges.

Using a decorator's bag with an open star tip, pipe a line of white frosting at the very peak of the roof to connect the graham crackers. You may also want to go around the edges of the graham crackers as well so you can stick candy all around the roof's edges.

Continue to pipe lines of frosting around all the edges of the house and then decorate the cake as you would a gingerbread house using your choice of candies.

Polar Bear

SERVES 10 TO 12

Pans

Muffin pan
1 (2.5-quart) glass mixing bowl

Cake

1 (15.25-ounce) box cake mix,
   any flavor
1 recipe Vanilla Buttercream
   Frosting (page 14) or 1
   (16-ounce) can white frosting
1 tube blue or red decorating
   icing
1 tube black decorating icing
   or gel
Red rope licorice or 1 tube red
   decorating icing or gel
2 Oreo cookies
2 blue M&Ms
Red Fruit by the Foot

Preheat oven to 350 degrees. Prepare 3 muffin cups and the bowl with nonstick cooking spray.

Make cake mix according to package directions. Fill the 3 muffin cups ²⁄₃ full with batter. Pour remaining batter into the bowl. Bake for 17–20 minutes, or until a toothpick inserted into 1 of the cupcakes comes out clean; remove from oven and cool for 10 minutes before turning out of pan. Continue baking the cake another 25 minutes, or until a wooden skewer inserted into the center comes out clean; remove from oven. Cool cake in bowl for 10 minutes, and then invert and cool completely on a wire rack.

On a large serving platter or foil-wrapped board, lay the round cake flat-side-down and place 2 cupcakes at the top to create the bear's face and ears.

Frost the sides and tops of the 2 cupcakes as well as the rest of the cake with white frosting. Slice off the top of the remaining cupcake and place it slightly below the middle

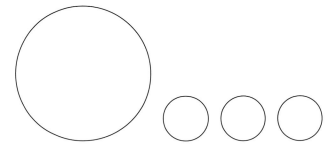

Continued . . .

Polar Bear

center of the bear's head to create the nose. Frost and blend the sides of the cupcake into the bear's face with white frosting.

Using the blue or red icing, fill in a circle in the middle of each ear. Using the black icing or gel, pipe a nose on the cupcake top. Use red rope licorice or red icing to make the mouth.

Separate the cookies and place just above the nose, with the cream filling face up, to make the eyes. Use the M&Ms to make the pupils. Form a bow tie out of the Fruit by the Foot and place below his mouth as shown in the photo.

Santa

SERVES 10 TO 12

Pan

9 x 13-inch pan

Cake

1 (15.25-ounce) box cake mix, any flavor

1 recipe Vanilla Buttercream Frosting (page 14) or 1 (16-ounce) can white frosting, divided, ½ left white

About ¾ cup light pink or peach frosting

About ¼ cup red frosting

1 tube black decorating icing or gel

Shredded coconut or mini marshmallows

1 tube red decorating icing or gel

Preheat oven to 350 degrees. Prepare pan with nonstick cooking spray.

Make cake mix according to package directions. Pour batter evenly into pan. Bake for 27–32 minutes, or until a toothpick inserted in the center comes out clean; remove from oven. Cool cake in pan for 10 minutes, and then invert and cool completely on a wire rack.

Cut the cake according to the diagram. Place 1 of the triangle pieces at the top of a large serving platter or foil-wrapped board to create Santa's hat. Place the rectangle piece underneath for Santa's face, and the remaining triangle below that to make his beard.

Frost Santa's entire beard white, along with a strip of white at the bottom of his hat. Frost a white circle at the top of his hat. Frost his face pink or peach and his hat red. Using a decorator's bag with a small round tip and black frosting, pipe on Santa's eyes and nose. Finish decorating by pressing coconut or marshmallows all over the white frosting; add Santa's mouth using the red icing.

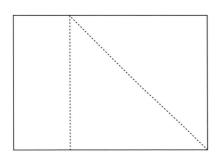

About the Author

Melissa Barlow is a cookbook author and a freelance writer and editor. She also has formal training in cake decorating. She lives in the Salt Lake City area with her husband and three children.

Metric Conversion Chart

Volume Measurements		Weight Measurements		Temperature Conversion	
U.S.	**Metric**	**U.S.**	**Metric**	**Fahrenheit**	**Celsius**
1 teaspoon	5 ml	1/2 ounce	15 g	250	120
1 tablespoon	15 ml	1 ounce	30 g	300	150
1/4 cup	60 ml	3 ounces	90 g	325	160
1/3 cup	75 ml	4 ounces	115 g	350	180
1/2 cup	125 ml	8 ounces	225 g	375	190
2/3 cup	150 ml	12 ounces	350 g	400	200
3/4 cup	175 ml	1 pound	450 g	425	220
1 cup	250 ml	2 1/4 pounds	1 kg	450	230